A MIND UNLEASHED

Quenten Lamar Howard

A Mind Unleashed

Kingdom Builders Publications

Library of Congress Control Number 2013921982
ISBN: 978-0-578- 14627-0

Photography
LH Photography "Just Pose"

Cover Designer
Visions Made Plain
LoMar Designs

Illustrator
Rorrie Travis
Aleese Black

Editors:
Kingdom Builders Publications

Printed in USA

Go to our website:
www.kingdombuilderspublications.com

This Book Belongs to

Acknowledgement

Lashanda Howard (Mom) –

Thanks for bringing me into this world. I would never be the man that I am today without you. Through the craziness of lost balls in my life, you have molded from a kid into the strong respectable and dedicated man I am today. Thank you.

Leroy Howard (Dad) –

The photographer that takes the best pictures in the world "Stay humble Stay alive". "It's hard on the yard."

Brandon (Brother) –

Thanks for giving me the motivation to always be better than I was yesterday.

"They didn't know you before and they don't know you now"

"No two trips"

Louise Smith (Publisher) –

Thank you for reaching out to me and helping me step by step through this entire process.

"Let's Go! "We're moving...We're here!"

Justice –

Thanks for inspiring me to keep chasing the stars and showing me that if you are true to yourself the best people in your life will stay around no matter the distance. Stay safe and come back soon, nothing but love for you forever and a day, still counting the days. The next World cup, the Vikings Game, and Hawaii is waiting for us.

"Remember keep calm and don't hang up."

Rorrie –

The illustrator that helped me paint the pictures of the thoughts that were in my mind. My brother from another mother
"Rada Rada Shaba dada", "stay away from them Spider webs you know what happens when we don't."

Sheybrele –

Thanks for being there during that crazy senior year. Thanks for opening my book that one day and telling me I could do something amazing with my writing. Don't let anything stop you from being great and remember you can do anything even when it looks like you can't.
"Dime Five"

The Crew –

Thank you all for being there for the good the bad and the ugly I know that we are all going to do something great with our lives, see you all in the future.

Colin –

We are both going to be great one day riding around in the nicest cars and looking stronger anyone out there.
"Keep putting that work in"

Taylor –

Thanks for showing me how to keep my ankles from being broke by the basics. My other brother "Crusty" you may be taller but I am still better man don't go ghost again man.

Other People That Changed Me –

To all the people that came in and out of my lives you also had an effect on my life whether it was positive or negative I thank you all the same because if it wasn't for you I wouldn't be the person I am now. If I could go back in time I would do it all over again because I know that this is the destiny that had been waiting for me my entire life.

Phase 1

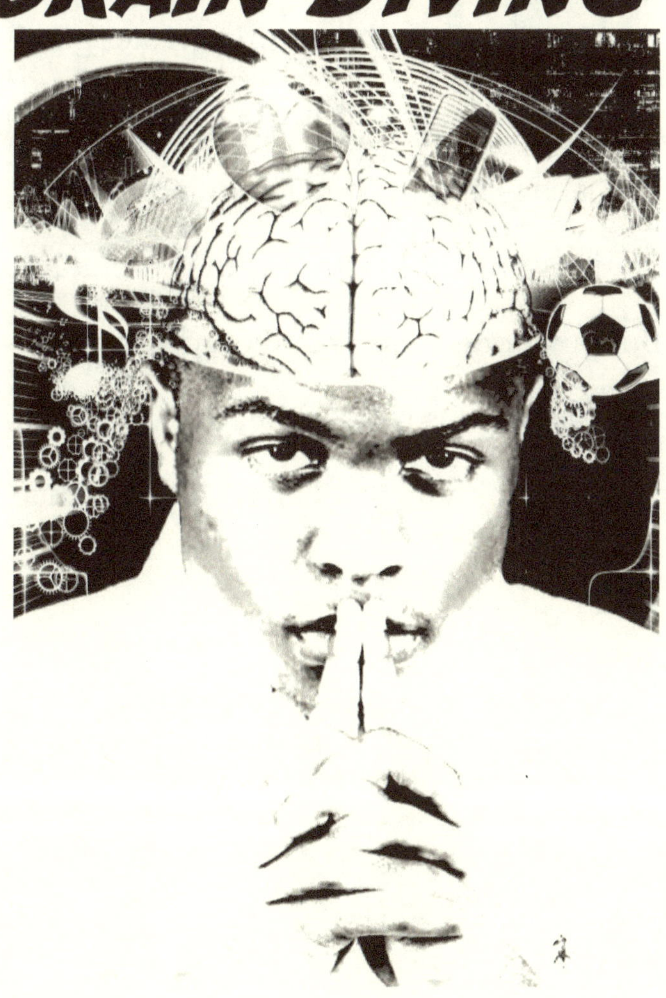

IN MY MIND

As I stand on my own locked away thinking

My deepest thoughts I would be reading

In my mind everything was so misunderstood

Living a life fighting for a greater good

Looking forward trying to find my destiny

Moving above and beyond looking for the best in me

Negativity surrounds me like the air that I breathe

But power holds strong like a positive disease

My mind is impossible to understand

But just know that I am a different man

YOU AND ONLY YOU

The mind works in mysterious ways

Life is like the oceans and we are the waves

Just floating around trying to find sand

A place to plant our feet and land

A place to think and plan

On the road to making it

A lot of us try without faking it

Thinking trying not to forsake it

Waking up every day seeing our future and taking it

Like a blazing fire

We work for what we desire

But of course there are those who say stop

Who put cuffs on our dreams like a cop

We come into this world without much knowledge

So yea we listen

Without much resistance

But were not done that's just the beginning

Of the first ending.

Every day we try to dot the I's and cross our t's

Hoping to keep everything in order

A bad smell comes in from haters like a bad odor

The disgust

The mistrust

The abuse

The misuse.

Stabbed in the back by the blades like shark teeth

Piercing the mind and changing the thoughts of the unknown

Even though the future is not shown

We feel alone

Left to fend for yourself

Going on without help

But I got a clue

That isn't true

It's like a verb

It's not about what you heard

And not about what happens to you

But it's all about what you do

Because let's face it no one controls your actions

Except you

No one takes the chances and tries to reach your dreams

Except you

No one is fighting through all the obstacles

Except you

If you haven't gotten it by now understand it starts with you

You have to decide who you hang around You have to figure out who is going to pick you up when you're down

You have to get past the obstacles in your way

You have to try to succeed everyday

No one controls how you play

It's all about what you do and what you say

CLOSER I GET

The closer I get
The more I remember and miss
So many things like that one special kiss
My words were gone speechless
For the fact I couldn't believe this
I was more shocked than you think
Then I felt my heart sink
Look at you I was at a loss for words
Wanting to say something you never heard
Taking you out it was like a dream
I felt too close to ever leave
The times I see your face or hear that song
I just pause as if something's wrong
Was it really true?
Is there anything else I can do?
I want to know how you feel
Is it just me making a big deal?
Your heart decides what it truly wants
Not knowing my mind it truly haunts
Just one step closer today
Seems like I can't get you anyway
But you sit there and don't bat an eye
Am I just some stupid guy
So I ask why
Should I even bother and try

FREE ME

Before you there was just me

Nothing more I was free

Just me

That's all I could see

It was fine

The world was mine

Then in came you

I didn't know what to do

I was dumb I looked like a fool You

were playing a game just for school

I wanted it to be us

No I wanted it to be we

Not more just us you see

More than one less than three

That was all I need

But I was dumb and stuck in greed

HOW DO...

How do I change
How do I make it right
How do I keep you in range
How do I stay in your sight
How do I breathe
How do I stand
How do I get you to see
How do I get you to understand
How do you feel when IM not there
How do you see it
How do I know you care
How do we not split
How do we walk
How do we, with no words
How do we talk
How do we like small birds
How do we give a smile
How do we joke like it's alright
How do we leave each other like caring is out of style

LOVE IS

Love is used to fast

Love is made to smooth

Is love really there?

Do we even care

Love is for the only

Love is for the one

Passion goes to some

But love is saved for the special

Love is with your heart

Love is with your soul

There is one heart for a reason

Your brain is made for thinking

Love is to be decided by your heart

Love is not to be chosen by your brain

Do I really know what love is?

NO GOING BACK

There's no way to change what has been done

From the moonlight to the sun

I hope you enjoyed your past

Because it just might be your last

There is no going back

So get back on track

Will it make it any clearer

To see yourself in a mirror

This is not the ending

Just a new beginning

THERE'S MORE

There's more
Some don't see the differences
On the outside a strong fast person
To others just another laugh
There's more
A heart filled with Care
A passion for love
Respect for the ones around him
There's more
Only seen as a box
No knowledge taken
Stuck in one place because of the past
There's more
A future so bright no one is ready to believe
The flash of random to splash into the day
A smile waiting for all
There's more
Taken as a joke when he speaks
Sees the world differently
So different he doesn't find a spot
But wait there's more
But should there be less

THOUGHTS OF UNKNOWN

There is this thought
A thought inside my mind that haunts
That taunts me and screams terror The
darkness has its own power
Coming closer to being too much to bear
These thoughts are unfair
The thoughts left in the air
Leaving me without a care
Over thinking everything
Underestimating nothing
These thoughts carry fear
But these thoughts are unclear
The size of a shadow from a solar eclipse
Covering everything around me
These thoughts try to take over
But these thoughts I must uncover
These thoughts cover mind
Makes me just that much more blind
These thoughts have no control

TIC TOC

Tic Toc…

The time passing us bye and bye

Don't know what to do should I even bother to try

Tic Toc…

Here we go again another day I spend

Not being around a great longtime friend

Tic Toc…

The time comes and goes

But with every moment passing by IM taking almighty blows

Tic Toc…

How long do we play this game of chance

All I want is the last dance

Tic Toc…

I am slowly running out of time

No more can be done can we just leave the past behind

Tic Toc…

TIME LOST

The time lost the time is gone

Our time we had was just so fun

Every time with you it was just so great

Now it seems I showed up too late

Everything happened after just one game

It blew up and nothing was the same

There is so much left to gain

Why didn't I stay in my lane

It all came from that kiss

Holding my arms around you I will miss

Us together it just clicked

Now I feel so sick

I can't take back what was said

Now I just sit and lay in bed

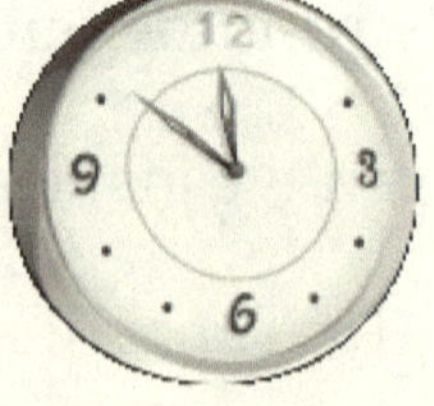

WHERE DID IT COME FROM?

I just caught a feeling like no other
Going beyond and past my brother
Where did it come from?
Something said I had more
Something said I had to score
Where did it come from?
The adrenaline flowing through my veins
The power inside of my brain
Where did it come from?
Deep inside my heart
Telling me I can start
Where did it come from?
Something in my mind
Telling me to get up and enjoy the ride
Where did it come from?
This deep seeded passion
That's there and forever lasting
Where did it come from?
The drive and determination
It's crazy this unknown inspiration
Where did it come from?

Phase Two

A HEART CHASING MEMORIES

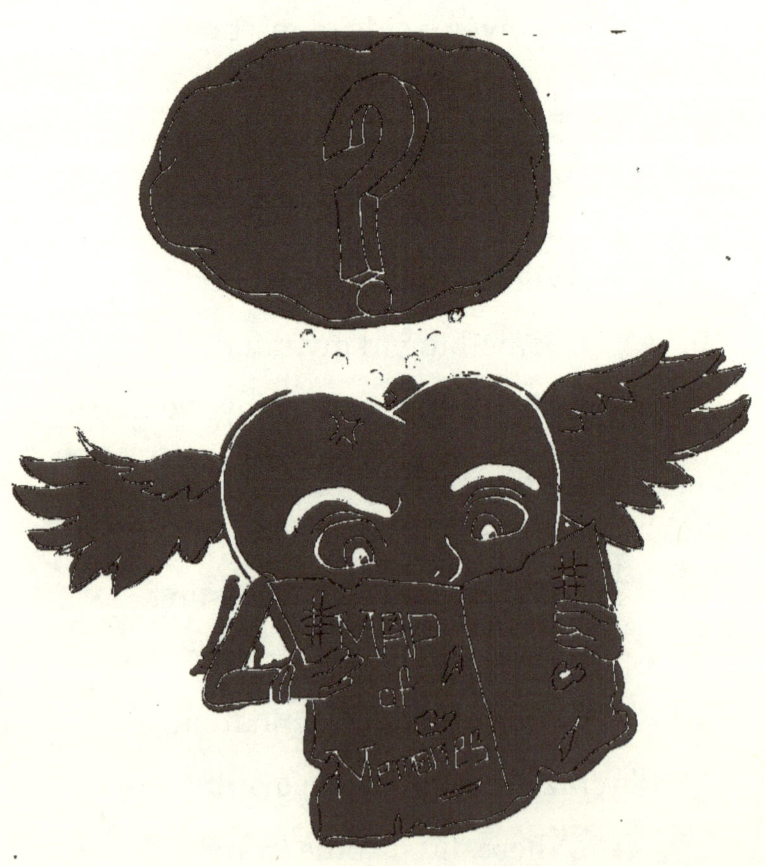

CROSS COUNTRY LOVE

They say distance makes the heart grow fonder
In my eyes it makes the mind wander
No matter how much you try not to
You still want to know what you could do
The miles that a person must travel just to be together
Even though it might not last forever
It's something you can't control
Your arms I want to have and to hold
Highways, lands and distances are in the way
Too far away to hear what she can say
She lives all the way in another state
Thinking about her could be a huge mistake
The heart wants what the heart wants without a care
The brain is stuck creating this vision out of thin air
She is so far away
But in my heart and mind she will stay.

BLIND LOVE

Days go by and by

And you're the only one that catches my eye

Reaching out to you but I'm losing every time

You kind-a-know but you're still missing the sign

Only you is who I am trying to find

Not seeing you I feel blind

Never knowing when I will see you again breaks my heart

All I see is you and this is just the start

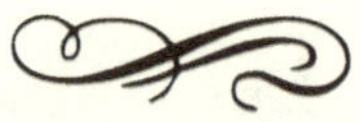

FAR AWAY

I am so far away

But when I close my eyes

It's only you that crosses my mind

I'm done. I tried to quit

But every time I blink

Your face shows up and I sink

Just to think

This is it.

Does it fit

Should I quit

So far away my heart has split

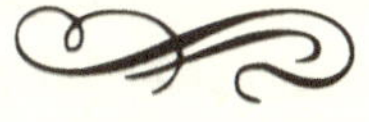

HEART BEAT

The pounding in my chest

Beating without a clue

Stays calm when at rest

Races when I see you

The rhythm changes from my hands

Down to my feet

My life can be changed in a moment's notice

Affected by those held closest

One moment of shock

Has my heart running at speeds

No time to mark left on the clock

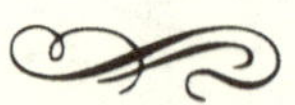

HER SMILE

One smile can be happy

A smile is something you don't generally see

Her smile could light the day

To make her laugh with every word I say

That smile is like a dream

With one thought not missing a thing

HOW MUCH I CARE

This isn't fair

How much I care

All I can do is stop and stare

I want to sit you down in a small chair

Just to show you how much I care

Take away all your hair

From the bottom of your feet to the top of your hair

All I want to do is show you how much I care

LOST CATCH

Days go by

And you are the only one that catches my eye

Reaching out to you but I'm losing every time

You kind of know but you are still missing the sign

Only you is who I am trying to find

Not seeing you I feel blind

Never knowing when I will see you again break my heart

All I see is you and this just the start

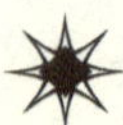

LAST BREATH

The clock is ticking

There is not much time left

To you I give my last breath

My life will not be spent in remorse

I may have gone and run the course

Whether in life or some other sport

I wish to make my wrongs right in some sort

My time may be short without a clue

But my last breath is what I give to you

My life is a total contradiction

And you were my favorite addiction

I hope you will listen

For my last breath you will be missing

I take this chance and say

You have my last breath as long as you stay

LOST LOVE

I loved her more than she ever knew
Went so far I didn't know what to do
It was above and beyond how much I cared
So amazing the times we shared
I must confess
I am the one that made the mess
All I want is a reason
For your unknown treason
This changed my whole life
Dealing with pain and strife
Taken away all in an instant
I know that I am truly going to miss this
My feeling s for you will never change
As long as you are in my range
I will always have you in my heart
From the end all the way from start
I had you up and above
But it seems you were just a lost love

MY LAST NIGHT

Back when we were close
You were the one I loved most
My last night it seemed true
I was weak a very blue
I looked in your face and seen that you cared
Remembering all the fun times we shared
I thought back to the ball
Yea we had it all
Then I thought to prom
Now that was the bomb
Who knew after that I would be alone
I still miss everything we had Leaving
you I felt so bad
I had a few fears
When I left and saw your tears
I just want another time to enjoy your sight
Just one more night

PASSION

When you care about something enough you do

Everything you can to win it

But obviously you don't get it

How can you stand there and tell me to quit it

When you are not even in it

I am working with a passion

Greater than anything in higher fashion

I'm ready for the day to cash in

Just so I can see your reaction

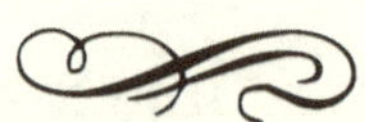

POEM OF HER

Beautiful, smart and strong

Member of the crew

Lover of the red rose

Who feels power

Who feel courage

Who feels taken

Who needs nothing more than the ground she stands on

Who gives their heart to the few

Who gives their smile to light the world

Who gives their all at work

Who fears losing her food

Who fears losing the ones she has closest

Who fears falling for the same thing twice

Who would hopefully like to see me

SOLAR BEAUTY ECLIPSE

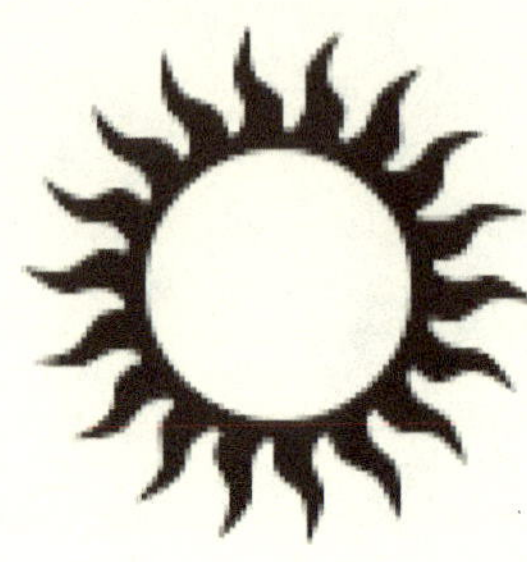

The sun is brighter than the moon

And I hope to see you soon

The sun is your beauty

The moon is your pain

I will look so sue me

Your smile holds my brain

With you there's more to see

Don't hide your beauty

Behind your pain

The sun is brighter than the moon

And I hope to see you soon

THAT GIRL

Every time I see her
A pause in time A
lost for words
No words can express how I feel
Her eyes so beautiful
Her smile lights up my day
Her laugh so soft and so sweet
Her presence makes me weak
One day I hope to be closer
Want to be closer than all
A life time to spend with this girl
Could only be a dream
I sit back watching
Because of not knowing what to say
Does she even care?
How does she feel?
My heart is hers to take
That girl will be on my mind forever and a day

THIS WON'T END HERE!

This won't end here
It's like you hit me with a sphere
Without you there is nothing left for me to gain
All I feel is heart ache and pain
To me it just seems to be a game
All I can do is sit back and stare
I remember your sweetest smell
My heart racing but you can never tell
It feels like I am starting to go insane
All I want to do is keep you warm in the pouring rain
Before this happen you were more than a great friend
This is not how I want it to end
I see you in every place
My feelings I must hold in a smaller case
Back then was the best, our greatest time
It was sweeter than a sip of lemon lime
Now there's nothing but an awkward silence
All because of a random act of kindness
Sometimes I ask why I am still here
But again I say this won't end here

YOU STOPPED ME

There's this thing that stops me

Your smile: it shocks me

Your eyes: they lock me

Your hands: they rock me

Your thoughts: they block me

I tried to show you

But I guess I don't know you

I thought I told you

I want to hold you

There's much more but I can't with the cold you

A MOMENT

A moment for me

A moment for you

A moment I see

A moment I knew

The moment you win

The moment you lose

The moment of highs

The moment of lows

There isn't a moment left alone

There isn't a moment left unchecked

But one day there will be a moment of one last breath

A ROSE FOR HER

Roses are red violets are blue

Every time I think it's always about you

My time with you is always fun

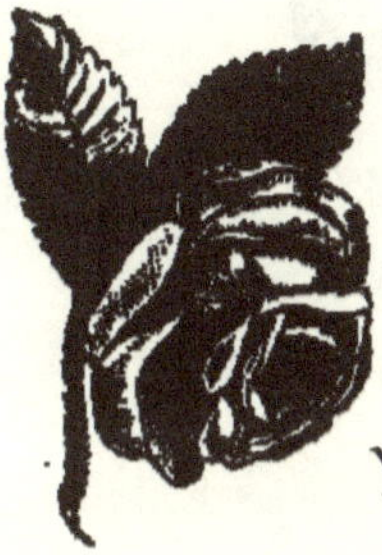

To me you are brighter than the sun

Where do I start

You already know you hold my heart

I have told you again and again

That I want to be your man

So as I stand in this crazy place

While I'm with you my heart beats at a faster pace

Let me make this very clear

When I see you I smile from ear to ear

Now tell me, how that sounds

Before you answer let me break it down

Phase Three

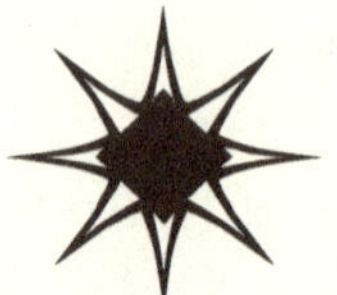

HOUR GLASS TICKING

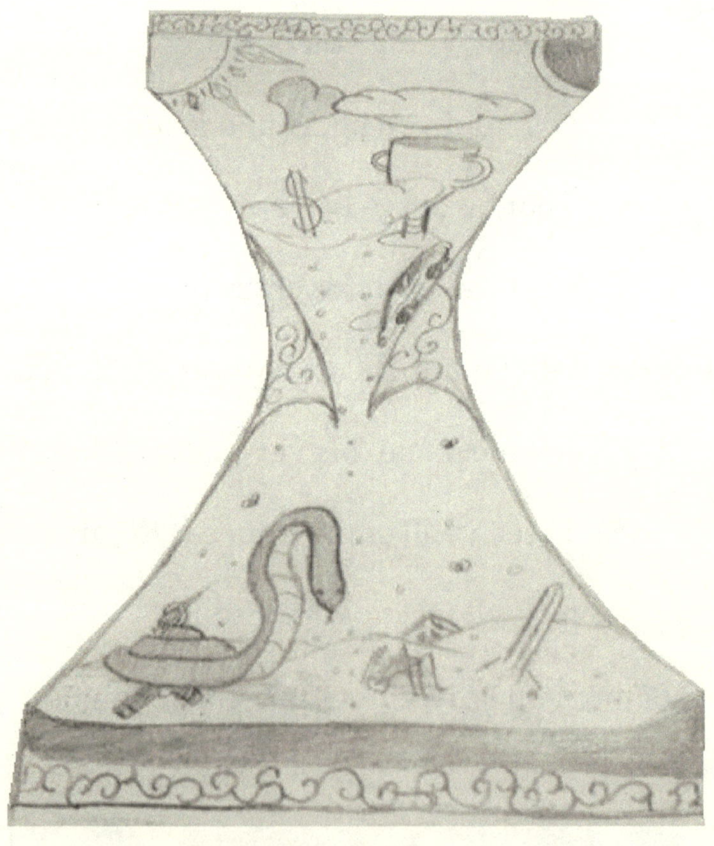

RISE OF LIFE IN ME

I'm Tired

Tired of being told I can't do something

Tired of being told I'm too slow

Tired of being told I'm too small

Tired of being told I'm to week

I'm Tired

Tired of being looked at as something unworthy

Tired of standing on my own two feet and no one having my back

Tired of fighting every day and not seeing results

Tired of taking tests that don't connect with my future

I'm Tired

Tired of being pushed around

Tired of getting up to be knocked back down

Tired of standing up for my dreams just to be told no

Tired of aspiring to do something that people think is impossible

I'm Tired

Tired of having to prove people wrong

Tired of people taking me as a joke

Tired of feeling low

Tired of not knowing where to go

I'm Tired enough to sleep

Tired enough to dream

Tired enough to rise

Tired enough to live

Tired enough for me

I Sleep

Sleep to get away from what haunts me

Sleep to get peace

Sleep to relax

Sleep to look back

I Sleep

Sleep to see what I can do

Sleep to move faster

Sleep to grow

Sleep to get stronger

I Sleep

Sleep to be worthy

Sleep to get results

Sleep to be amazing

Sleep to get power

I Sleep

Sleep to feel free

Sleep to be me

Sleep to create a vision

Sleep to get closer to my future

I Sleep

Sleep enough to dream

Sleep enough to Rise

Sleep enough to live

Sleep enough for me

My Dream

Dreams to be great

Dreams to inspire others

Dreams to create hope

Dreams to reach my goals

My Dream

Dreams to do above and beyond what other people expect

Dreams of a greater future

Dreams of a loving family

Dreams of glorious success

My Dream

Dreams of being unstoppable

Dreams of never being told no

Dreams of being good enough

Dreams of reaching more than what others expect

My Dream

Dreams of soaring to new heights

Dreams of destroying the obstacles in my way

Dreams of being untouchable

Dreams of being mesmerizing

My Dream

My Dream is to rise

My Dream is to live

My dream is for me

I Rise

Rise above those who have doubted me

Rise to the occasion

Rise beyond belief

Rise to continue my journey

I Rise

Rise to lift up ones around me

Rise to unknown limits

Rise to unknown limits

Rise to past the stars and create my own galaxy

Rise to my own universe

I Rise

Rise to the opportunities knocking at my door

Rise to take the shots not yet taken

Rise to achieve a greater destiny

Rise to find new abilities

I Rise

Rise to move closer

Rise to see those left behind

Rise to meet the next challenge face to face

Rise to take control of my world

I rise

Rise not to be tired

Rise not to sleep

But I Rise to live

I Rise for me

I Live

Live for the ones who came before me

Live for the ones I love

Live to be remarkable

Live to do things beyond belief

I Live

Live to throw caution to the wind

Live to take control of what is rightfully mine

Live to surpass what has happened in history

Live to create my own records

I Live

Live to get closer move faster and get stronger

Live for the next day

Live for what I worked for

Live for the game we call life

I Live

Live for the look on the faces of those who doubted

Live to hold up my own trophy

Live to fight to be amazing

Live to do what hasn't been done

I Live not to be tired

Not to sleep

But I Live

I Live for me

BURNING DESIRES

The fire in my eyes
The heat of my anger
Hearing these lies
Feeling left in danger
The steam flying out of my ears
Ignoring all that surrounds me
Going past all killing my fears
Not worrying about anything around me
My mind filled with rage
My body filled with fire
IM left feeling trapped in a cage
All I want is my hearts deepest desire
Built up into great intensity
Pull back and on lockdown
The reason for it not what it was meant to be
Left alone to win my own crown

FIGHT FOR LIFE

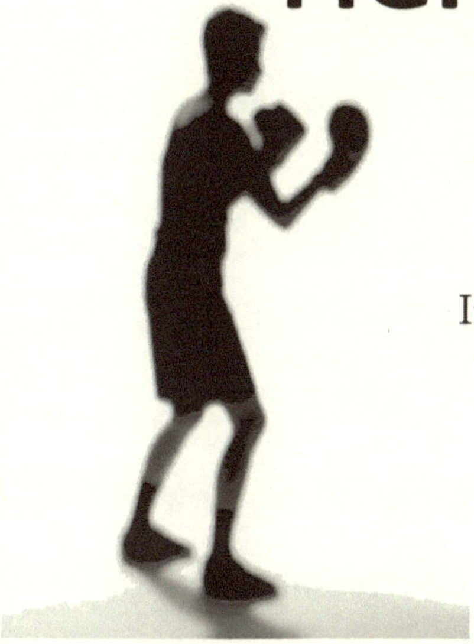

That faithful day coming to the light

No thought given

It was amazing a life ready to be taken

Yours to be achieved

The gift that GOD gave you

So unreal you can't believe

Your only way to go forth and try to succeed

Although the world you enter is calm and shallow

You still must fight

Oh yes fight

Fight for the great

Fight for your own

Fight for your goals

Fight for your soul

For there is no one yet on your side

QUIET

Way to calm

Simpler than the look of my palm

When everything so good and feels so fine

Still something left for us to find

It is a very rude awakening

Makes you think about what you are forsaking

The reason for it left unknown

Everyone gone and you're on your own

Not how one should live their life

Walking around stuck in strife

There is so much I rather do

But now I'm stuck just looking at you

There's so much guilt there's so much shame

Everything going wrong being left in vain

You on your own will never know this

Now all has gone and you are left feeling hopeless

REMEMBER THE TIME

Remember the time

Playing games out in the street

Making moves right to the beat

Remember the time

Everybody was trying to make cash

Then first time you ran the forty yard dash

Remember the time

We were all young

Not a care in the world just having fun

Remember the time

Our imagination could take us any where

It didn't matter our brains didn't care

Just look back and

Remember the time

THE TRUTH

The Truth
It's not about believing what you see
It's about believing what you mean
I'm talking about your dreams
That goes with everything
The truth
Yea it's hard to find
It blows my mind
That all the signs
Are so unkind
It leaves everyone blind
The truth
We have to get a clue
To tell the story of what we have been through
The truth
Why lie
When you can't look me in my eye
Besides
You can tell the truth or lie
And end up six feet under and die
So I'm going to ask one more time
Make sure you're not feeding me another line
The Truth?

IS IT POSSIBLE?

Is it possible?
How can I stop the unstoppable?
That's sounds improbable
We are quick to flea our dreams in haste
Too scared to look destiny in the face
It's a disgrace
How some discriminate by race
Even though we run the same pace
But moving on looking for good grace
It's like playing spades and having an ace
But too scared to play it because of what someone might say
I will not let someone else decide my fate
Because they are just spending nights up real late
Finding new ways to create hate
I know some of you can relate
Telling people they need to quit
Looking at their dreams and covering them in spit
Just because they are trying to get
What you missed
Just because you slipped
Doesn't mean they did
So stop acting like a kid
And asking if it's possible
Be unstoppable
Make it probable
Because anything is possible

HIDING LIFE

Back in the day I was a kid

And like any other kid I had dreams hopes and open opportunity.

As a kid I looked up to people

Not only because of their successes

But because I was smaller

Everybody I looked up too yea they were taller.

As I move through life I learned my lessons

While at the same time people asked me these crazy questions.

They said when you grow up what do you want to be.

I looked at them with a straight face

I said what you mean

I want to be me.

You see in my mind I was happy

I had a mother that loved me and a proud daddy.

Again my teachers asked me

What I wanted to do with my life.

I say why ask again

I'm only five

How can I decide?

Being five

I thought life was just learning to be alive

But later I learned it's about trying to survive.

Now I wasn't any ordinary kid

In no ordinary family

I had a deep passion

That no one could understand me

Shoot it was hard for people to handle me.

As a military child I learned army values

Like respect and disciplined.

But in the end it was like no one was listening.

As if no one could hear me

Or I wasn't speaking clearly.

It was like we moved yearly.

Home…

Yea everybody had one.

But honestly I felt like a bullet loaded in a handgun.

Every time I get calm stable

And reach my hearts desires

It was

Tick

Tick

Tick

BOOM SHOTS FIRED!

It was time for change

It was like a president's campaign

Everything I was told

It was a lie

All I could do is sit

And ask why

Again and again

I moved and I moved

I went where I went

And I got what I got

A place for me

I had no such spot.

A place

For me to live my dreams.

You know

Do my own things

But I like any other kid would be denied

Every time I tried

Again I move on

And try to do my best
Whether I had more
Or I had less
Everywhere I went
It was the same old thing
By this time I was ten so yea I learned a little bit.
So when I got to class I knew what I would get.
I would get another teacher
That thought she was a preacher.
Asking the same old questions
Trying to teach the same old lessons.
But I'm not stressing
I understand that this was a blessing
I took on the world one step at a time.
It blew my mind.
The truth
Is what I wanted to find.
What I found out
Was that I was truly blind
I was supposed to be kind
Not because of the obvious signs
But because of the possible fines.

In life we have to stay in line
But repeatedly it hit my mind
There was never any logic
The more teachers spoke
The more I heard nonsense.
My teachers told me to make a decision
This was just another way for them to ask a question
Ignore me and not listen
It was like a bad mission.
As I got older
I learned more and more things
By this time I was thirteen
My eyes were still open
Yea I still had dreams
It was a beautiful thing.
I would start to have a goal
You know as a kid once you hit thirteen
Guess what
You are starting to get old.
Things became routine
Like my laundry and washing everything.
But as I was getting ready for my life I realized

That my future

Was apparently known by these losers

Yes I mean my teachers

They were the ones that told me who I would be.

Every time I told them about my dream

All they could think is why it couldn't be.

When they said this they were losing me

If I didn't back down from what I wanted to do

They gave me a clue

They compared me to everyone else

Like anyone else would do.

They gave me facts and figures…

That weren't true

They told me they went through what I went through

I said you don't have a clue.

They told me about a guy who apparently tried what I wanted to do

But he failed

And guess what news flash

If he failed

Apparently

I would too.

That's the world we live in
But really that's where the journey begins
Nothing makes sense
From end to end.
See when I got on my own
And was living alone
I felt a little grown
But again that was wrong
Oh look what a surprise
Life has left me mind blown.
There was this one thing I noticed
It was like a bad case of locust.
It hit my mind
And changed my focus.
I was looking at being alive
And enjoying life as a whole
But it's the same thing
And I'm getting old.
Somehow I had to make it clearer.
So I stopped looking at it as a whole big picture.
I went and thought back to my teachers
You remember those non-believers.

That kept asking me about life
This never made sense till I got a test back with a bad grade
I felt like my knowledge was about to fade.
You want to know what I got
Go ahead take a guess…
I thought I did my best
So when I got that paper back I lost my breath.
I looked at the paper
And took it to the teacher's desk
And asked him how I got an "F"
I'm telling you I tried my best He
looked at me
He went right and then left
He paused for a moment and took a deep breath.
He told me that this "F" was just a part of life.
And that's when I realized he was right.
After all this time
It got in my mind.
That life was just a lie
With something mixed in too make it look better
It's been that way always and forever.

But this is just my view

Living a life without the truth

Going on and on without a clue.

Back in the day I was a kid…

Wait that sounds like something I already did.

But that's life

Doing the same old thing

Again and again.

It's all a part of this vicious cycle

Like all the great athletes trying to chase the same old title.

Soon becoming someone else's idol

Just because of their unique style

. It causes people to become suicidal.

But for that to happen it would take a while

But that's what life is

It's dealing with the lie and adding something to hide it

. You can't deny it

We have all tried it

Moving on getting passed the violence

The lesson here is timeless.

Everyone goes through it

Even the mindless

. A kid like me had hopes dreams and open opportunity.

But a change happened

As I traveled through history

Yea it's a mystery

But now that I'm older it is oh so clear to me.

Everyone was hearing me

But that doesn't mean they were listening.

To get through life at some point I would be denied

No matter how hard I tried.

While at the same time

Very few people would be there standing by my side.

But again this is how I see the world in my eyes.

Everyone in the world was competing for the same old prize.

At the exact same time

So of course people told lies

That's how they lived their Lives.

Wow would you look at their lives

Guess what it's just more lies

But this time the world added a "V"

It was strange
I didn't understand it mentally
It blew my mind wait no this time
It affected me physically
Individually
It was killing me
But I figured it out willingly.
To have life
You had a lie
And you got an "F"
And failed miserably.
As if it was meant to be.
But to live
Means to go through life
And use your lie to find the "V"
And by "V"
I mean victory.
Now I can write my own history.
I can go through life
And die
Some would say that's suicide
But I'm going to let you decide.

I will continue on and work toward victory.

I can get stuck on the picture for what I see

Or I can take it for what I want it to be.

And go through life and think differently.

I choose mine mentally

No matter what life has given me

Soon the world will see

That I grew up to do what I always wanted to be

And yes that is me.

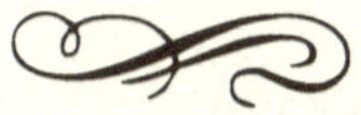

WHO I AM

This is who I am

Not trying to be something I'm not

When I was a kid I had big dreams

My imagination free to run wild

These things were oh so serious

People said I was delirious

Today I had my dreams from deep together

That's what will carry me forever

It's part of who I am

And always will be

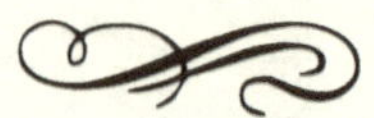

WHY DO YOU STILL SPEAK?

Roses are red

Violets are blue

To me you are dead and you have no clue

My life has been flipped

Turned upside down

Felt like you spit

And threw me on the ground

Don't try to speak

I no longer want to know

This isn't a game of hide and seek

You never really cared and it shows

Phase Four

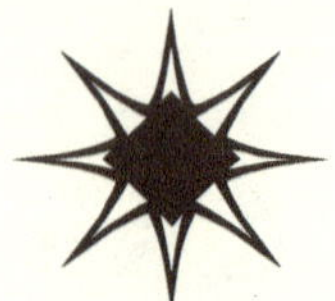

LION HEARTED

BLOOD SWEAT TEARS

One challenge will not stand in my way

I don't care what you say

As long as I am living

My all is what I will be giving

With mind body and soul

You have my all

Leaving the sweat on the field

Know what it takes to be real

With blood on my jersey

Not worrying about those that hurt me

Leaving the tears at home

If you trying to beat me don't come alone

You don't know what I have been through

How much I have to hold back just not to hit you

FEAR

Fear no such fear

The picture fading and not being clear

Fear in what I don't see

Falling from the highest tree

Losing all of me

Fear is a state of mind

My sight will go blind

Before I forget what was left behind

Fear isn't right

Losing the big fight

Going past you first sight

Fear is in all the above

That loss of the one you love

Fear is something I want none of

GAME

It's about that time the season approaching

The whistles blowing

The crowds roaring

Tying up the cleats on your feet

Making moves pulling everyone out there seat

HEART OF A LION

Follow through

No matter what tries to stop you

Heart of a lion

Just keep trying

There are things to gain

Drive through the pain

Give blood sweat tear

Go on with no fear

You have a Heart of a lion

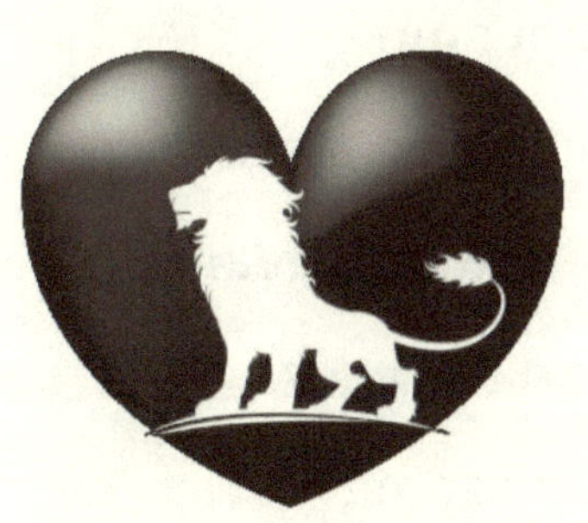

I KEPT GOING

My heart was pounding
My legs were hurting
But I kept going
I lost my breath
I was tired
But I kept going
I had no more to give
My body said stop
But I kept going
I didn't think I had anything left
People told me to stop
People said I couldn't do it
People said I wouldn't make it
But I kept going
No one gave me a chance
NO one believed in my dreams
No one had my back
But I kept going
I fell behind

I fell down

I was losing I couldn't see the finish line

There was no point in continuing on But

I kept going

Something said quit

Something said you're done

Something said it's over

Something said there is no more

But I kept going

My hands hurt

My feet hurt

It was too cold

It was too hot

It was too early

It was too late

But I kept going

There were other options

Other choices

Other opportunities

Other ways to go

But I kept going

STRONG TO WEAK

A muscle to a word
A feeling you never heard
My power is broken
For there are times when I am choking
The full body strain
To all the mental pain
I have the sight
But I have lost the light
There are so many emotions
I just need that one potion
To find a way pass this
I could make a list
My strength is too weak
I feel that I have reached the peak
I have seen a lot
Now I am trying to find that spot
Inside myself that makes me strong
For I have had it all along
Drop all the pain that makes me weak
Because I am too strong to be weak

THIS IS IT

This is it

Your last for what you want to get

You have to fight

Even though the weight isn't light

Give it your all

It's on you it's your call

Be weak or strong

One more rep and make it long

Get what you can get

Because this is it

GAME TRAINED

Everything I had wasn't enough

Going through it all trying to be tough

Apparently I wasn't ready

Trying to fight back and hold steady

I felt I was locked in like a safe

Working my hardest in this strange place

I played so hard my body tore

But they wanted so much more

Taking all the chances for the game

To end up losing all the same

It seemed like it was so clear

But now I wait another year

So again I train

In the cold, the Heat and the rain

THE HIDDEN PUSH

There is always someone in your corner
Waiting to lift you up and make you stronger
Even when you are down and feel alone
You are never on you are own Someone
is quietly watching your back Even
when you fall way off track
Digging deep down to find the strength
Allow nothing to knock you off and make you sink
Ready to fight against the best
Young and relentless trying to protect what's next's
Nearly impossible to find
Never letting you quit
Always helping you get what you get
No one can stand in your way
Because there are people pushing you everyday
Saying things to get you through
Helping you every day without a clue
Empty mind and soul
Your body moving to reach that goal
Battling all obstacles you can't see
Riding with you beyond belief
Encouraging you to follow your dream
Letting you live your crazy scheme

Exacting revenge on your enemy
Going to fight those who won't believe willingly
It has become a very common theme
And it seems
Your dreams
These things
Are unbelievable
Unachievable
To stop you is insane
Arguing with you can be the same
Yawning at the countless haters
Laughing at those past failures
Only you know what you are working for
Ready to take on the world with a fire hotter than the earth's core
Someone is quietly watching even if you don't know it
Hoping you make it even though they might not show it
Calmly watching you
Knowing how much you have been through
There are those people who give you advice
Those who ring the bell and show you what's right
Some may be far away
At the same time getting closer to you every day
Doing all they can

Energizing you to help you stand
Excepting you for who you are
Being an over watching star
Out there seeing your next move
Never letting you get out your groove
In some situations
You have to have the patience
Just to be your best
And wait to see it put to the test
That's how you can get justice
Keep shooting no matter how much you miss
Remember why you started in the first place
It's not about who is fast at the beginning of the race
Stopping at first base when you hit a home run makes no sense
So why give up when you know you don't have to give an inch
You're only as good as you allow yourself to be
So why wouldn't you go and chase your dreams
We go around the world searching
Hurting
Working
Lurking
Asserting
Alerting

But it's disturbing
How discouraging
That people are worrying
About the distant future
But need to work on today to change what's coming sooner
Sometimes you have to be optimistic
And not worry about what seems unrealistic
Forget about what's fact and fiction
Work as if you have a mission
Get out there and be the best
Allow yourself to beat the rest
Be phenomenal
Believe you will never fail its psychological
You have the final say
Ready for the day
Out there with a recipe
Racing toward your destiny
Intelligent enough to know what you want to do
Energetic enough to make it true
Refuse to quit
Absolutely no one can do what you did
Victory is what you are working for
Elude your past and open the next door
Never let anyone hold you down

Because in the end it will be you that is wearing the crown
There is always someone to help you
Even though they might not be next to you.
Collect on all the time you put in
Eliminate those negative thoughts that can't win
Learn from those life lessons
Illuminate the positives for they are blessings
Never give up those thoughts
At the end of the day that's all you got
At any moment you can be pushed down
Live your life and never stay on the ground
Eradicate anything that stands in your way
Xerox copy those moments in your mind that made you great
It's your life so live it
Stop crying and get it
Act like a colonel in the army
Stop worrying about if your phone needs charging
There are better things in life
Calm yourself and do what's right
Only you can change your future
Leave that sorry loser
Invent new ways to believe
NO one can stop you from what you want to achieve

It's your life
Your strife
Your destiny
Your recipe
Your beginning
Your ending
It's your mission
So listen
No matter how dark
There's always a spark
That's starts the fire
To your deepest desire
It only takes one clue
To get to what's true
Someone always has your back
So you never really get off track So
when you are alone by yourself
What happens to you also touches somebody else
And they are trying to feel what you felt

ABOUT THE AUTHOR

Quenten LaMar Howard - 1995

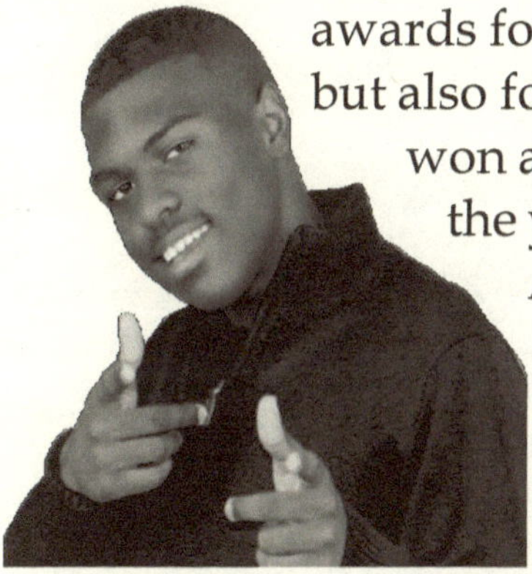

Quenten is a student athlete and has won numerous awards for his abilities not only on the field but also for his actions off the field. He has won awards such as all region Player of the year, National Athletic Scholar Award, and MVP of High School North South game. He studies at Winthrop University and is an Exercise Science Major aspiring to become a Physical Therapist in the future. He is dedicated to revolutionizing the way that people think and look at the world. Family and friends are a vital part of my life. Howard is a part of a military family. That alone has gained him opportunities to see new cultures which have broaden my scope of the world and his own personal style. "I was one of those kids that thought there were no limits to what I could go or do."

www.ingramcontent.com/pod-product-compliance
Lightning Source LLC
LaVergne TN
LVHW050938080826
845145LV00004B/1311

9780578146270